"I'd Just As Soon Kiss a Wookiee!"

THE QUOTABLE STAR WARS

"I'd Just As Soon Kiss a Wookiee!"

THE QUOTABLE STAR WARS

Stephen J. Sansweet

A Del Rey® Book
Ballantine Books • New York

A Del Rey® Book
Published by Ballantine Books

http://www.randomhouse.com

Library of Congress Catalogue Card Number: 96-96528

Interior design by Michaelis/Carpelis Design Assoc. Inc.

Manufactured in the United States of America

First Edition: October 1996

10 9 8 7 6 5 4

TABLE OF CONTENTS

INTRODUCTION

"Frankly my dear, I don't give a damn!"
"Here's looking at you, kid."
"The Force will be with you . . . always."

When a line from a film goes from screen to memory without pausing long enough to become a cliché, that's more than entertainment—that's the very essence of popular culture. And pop culture is one of the few things these days that provides us all at least a little shared identity. It makes the punch line of a joke funny, for example, without going through a laborious explanation. Thus, when a brown-robed and hooded actor with a white beard materializes on *Saturday Night Live* next to guest host Luke Perry, you start to snicker even before the inevitable, "Use the Force, Luke!"

The Star Wars Generation—those of us who grew up or matured with Star Wars on the brain—took great delight in the dialogue: the funny lines and the philosophical ones. In fact, these phrases keep surfacing under the most unlikely of circumstances: Walking with a friend to my car in a dark parking lot on the wrong side of town one evening, I couldn't help muttering, "I have a bad feeling about this." Or, searching for inspiration at the keyboard, I've been known to quietly mouth, "Help me, Obi-Wan Kenobi. You're my only hope."

It's not only our generation. A toy company president I know insists that we've passed on a "Star Wars gene" to the next generation. Fed by constantly rewound videos, youngsters across the world mimic the breathy tones of Darth Vader or the convoluted speech patterns of Yoda when they borrow a quote from the screen.

This book is an attempt to release at least some of the dialogue from the place where it's been locked up in my brain, thanks to George Lucas, Lawrence Kasdan, and Leigh Brackett. We've managed to fit in just about all of my favorites, except perhaps Han Solo's words of comfort to a wounded but recovering Luke Skywalker (". . . you look strong enough to pull the ears off a gundark") and Wedge Antilles's exclamation upon first seeing the Death Star ("Look at the size of that thing!").

Nope. I guess we got those, too.

—Steve Sansweet

A
Droid's
Lot in
Life

"**D**on't you call me a mindless philosopher, you overweight glob of grease!" —C-3PO to R2-D2

"**Y**ou'll be malfunctioning within a day, you nearsighted scrap pile!"

—C-3PO to R2-D2

"*N*o, I don't think he likes you at all. . . . I don't like you either."

—C-3PO to R2-D2

"*T*hat little droid and I have been through a lot together."

—Luke Skywalker (concerning R2-D2)

"*Y*ou must repair him! Sir, if any of my circuits or gears will help, I'll gladly donate them."

—C-3PO (concerning R2-D2)

"*W*e'll be destroyed for sure. This is madness!"

—C-3PO to R2-D2

"*W*e're doomed!"

—C-3PO to R2-D2

"*W*e'll be sent to the spice mines of Kessel or smashed into who-knows-what!" —C-3PO to R2-D2

"*W*e seem to be made to suffer. It's our lot in life."—C-3PO to R2-D2

"*T*hank the maker!"

—C-3PO

"*W*e don't serve their kind here!"

—Mos Eisley Cantina bartender

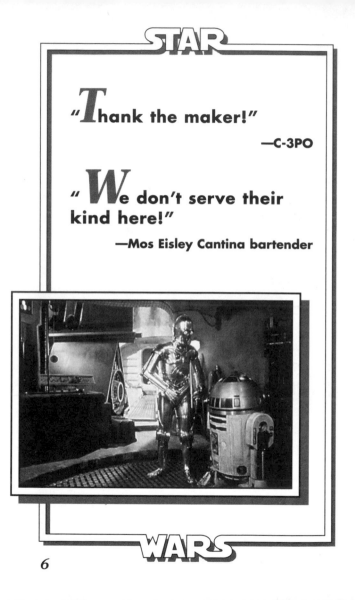

"*H*elp! I think I'm melting." —C-3PO

"*S*hut him up or shut him down!"

—Han Solo (concerning C-3PO)

"*A*rtoo says the chances of survival are seven hundred seventy-five . . . to one. Actually, Artoo has been known to make mistakes . . . from time to time."

—C-3PO to Princess Leia Organa and Chewbacca

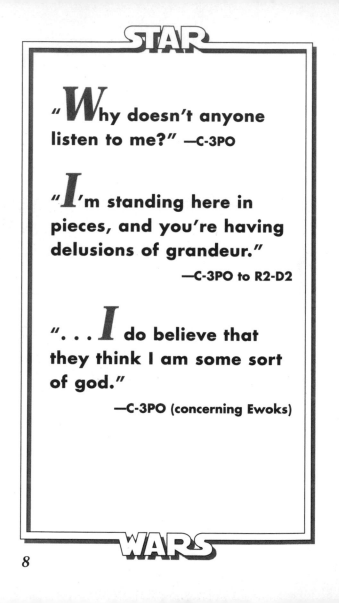

"*W*hy doesn't anyone listen to me?" —C-3PO

"*I*'m standing here in pieces, and you're having delusions of grandeur."

—C-3PO to R2-D2

". . . *I* do believe that they think I am some sort of god."

—C-3PO (concerning Ewoks)

YOU CAN TAKE THE FARMBOY OFF OF THE FARM...

"*Y*ou can waste time with your friends when your chores are done."

—Owen Lars to Luke

"*L*uke's just not a farmer, Owen. He has too much of his father in him." —Beru Lars

"*I* can't get involved. I've got work to do."

—Luke to Ben Kenobi

"*T*raveling through hyperspace isn't like dusting crops, boy!" —Han to Luke

"*I*'m not such a bad pilot myself!" —Luke to Han

"*Y*ou have taken your first step into a larger world." —Ben to Luke

"**A**ren't you a little short
for a stormtrooper?"

—Leia to disguised Luke

"**I**'m Luke Skywalker.
I'm here to rescue you."

—Luke to Leia

"**T**his is some rescue!"

—Leia

"*G*reat kid! Don't get cocky." —Han to Luke

"*I*t's not impossible. I used to bull's-eye womp rats in my T-sixteen back home." —Luke to Wedge Antilles

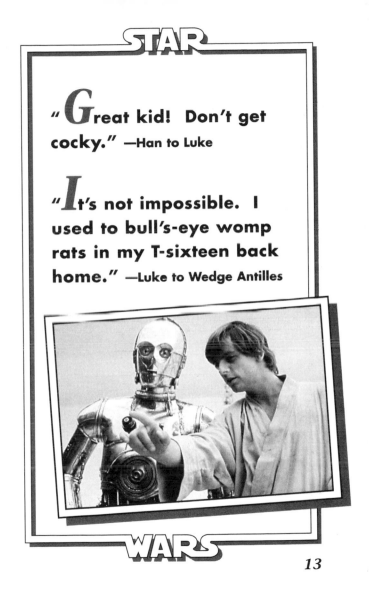

"*T*he Force is strong with this one!"

—Darth Vader (concerning Luke)

"**D**on't worry about Master Luke . . . He's quite clever, you know . . . for a human being."

—C-3PO to R2-D2

"**T**he son of Skywalker must not become a Jedi."

—Emperor to Vader

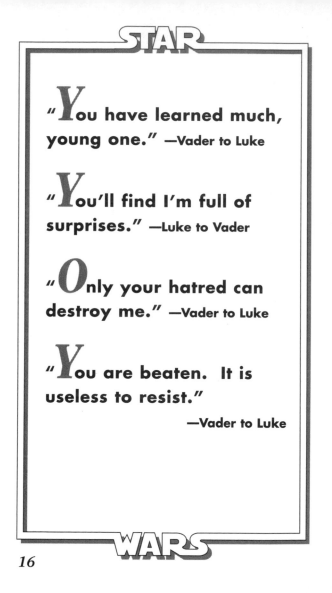

"*Y*ou have learned much, young one." —Vader to Luke

"*Y*ou'll find I'm full of surprises." —Luke to Vader

"*O*nly your hatred can destroy me." —Vader to Luke

"*Y*ou are beaten. It is useless to resist."

—Vader to Luke

"*L*uke's crazy. He can't even take care of himself, much less rescue anybody." —Han to Chewbacca

"*. . . I* warn you not to underestimate my powers." —Luke to Jabba

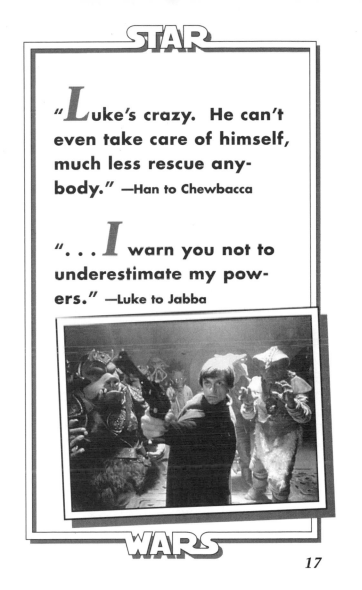

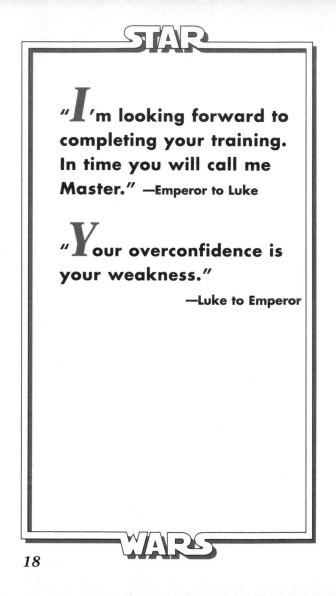

"**I**'m looking forward to completing your training. In time you will call me Master." —Emperor to Luke

"**Y**our overconfidence is your weakness."

—Luke to Emperor

THE
PROPER
PRINCESS

"*I* recognized your foul stench when I was brought on board!"

—Leia to Grand Moff Tarkin

"*C*harming to the last. You don't know how hard I found it signing the order to terminate your life." —Tarkin to Leia

"*I*nto the garbage chute, flyboy." —Leia to Han

"*W*hat an incredible smell you've discovered." —Han to Leia

"**W**onderful girl! Either I'm gonna kill her or I'm beginning to like her."

—Han (concerning Leia)

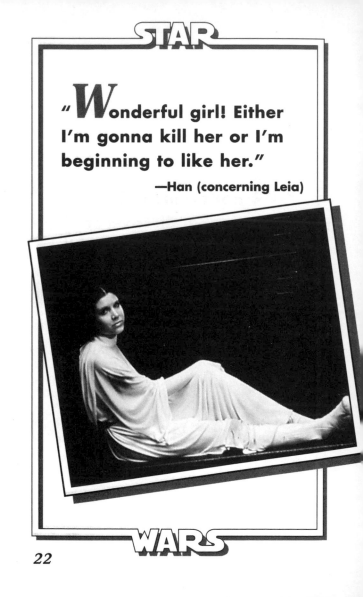

"*I* don't know who you are, or where you came from, but from now on, you do as I tell you. Okay?" —Leia to Han

"*W*hy, you stuck-up . . . half-witted . . . scruffy-looking nerf-herder!"

—Leia to Han

"*S*omeday you're gonna be wrong, and I just hope I'm there to see it."

—Leia to Han

"*Y*ou do have your moments. Not many of them, but you do have them." —Leia to Han

Everyone's Favorite Rogue

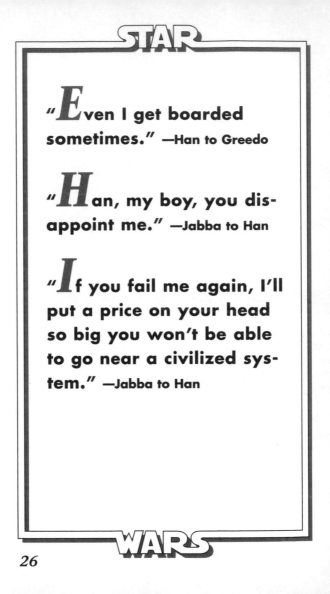

"*E*ven I get boarded sometimes." —Han to Greedo

"*H*an, my boy, you disappoint me." —Jabba to Han

"*I*f you fail me again, I'll put a price on your head so big you won't be able to go near a civilized system." —Jabba to Han

"*L*ook, Jabba, next time you want to talk to me, come and see me yourself. Don't send one of those twerps." —Han to Jabba

"*D*on't everybody thank me at once." —Han

"*I* prefer a straight fight to all this sneaking around." —Han

"*L*isten, if you were to rescue her, the reward would be . . . well, more wealth than you can imagine." —Luke to Han

"*I* don't know, I can imagine quite a bit."

—Han to Luke

"*I* take orders from just one person: Me!"

—Han to Leia

"*I*t's a wonder you're still alive." —Leia to Han

"*Y*ou know, sometimes I amaze even myself." —Han

"*W*hat good's a reward if you ain't around to use it?" —Han

"*H*ey, I knew there was more to you than money."

—Leia to Han

"*S*ir, the possibility of successfully navigating an asteroid field is approximately three thousand, seven hundred and twenty to one." —C-3PO to Han

"*N*ever tell me the odds!" —Han

"*Y*ou said you wanted to be around when I made a mistake; well, this could be it, sweetheart."

—Han to Leia

*"I*mpossible man."

—C-3PO (concerning Han)

*"H*is High Exaltedness, the great Jabba the Hutt, has decreed that you are to be terminated immediately." —C-3PO to Han

"*G*ood. I hate long waits." —Han to C-3PO

"*W*ell, short help is better than no help at all. . . ." —Han (concerning Ewoks)

"*I*'m rather embarrassed, General Solo, but it appears you are to be the main course at a banquet in my honor." —C-3PO to Han

THE
MILLENNIUM
FALCON

"*W*hat a piece of junk!"

—Luke

"*Y*ou've never heard of the *Millennium Falcon*? It's the ship that made the Kessel run in less than twelve parsecs."

—Han to Ben and Luke

"*Y*ou came in that thing? You're braver than I thought." —Leia to Han

"*D*on't worry, she'll hold together. . . . You hear me, baby? Hold together!" —Han to the *Falcon*

"*T*his bucket of bolts is never going to get us past that blockade." —Leia to Han

"*T*his baby's got a few surprises left in her, sweetheart." —Han to Leia

"*W*ould it help if I got out and pushed?"

—Leia to Han

"*W*e're in trouble!" —Han

"*S*he's the fastest hunk of junk in the galaxy."

—Lando Calrissian

OBI-WAN

"*H*elp me, Obi-Wan Kenobi. You're my only hope."

—Hologram of Princess Leia

"*O*bi-Wan? Now that's a name I haven't heard in a long time . . . a long time." —Ben Kenobi

"*I* was once a Jedi Knight, the same as your father." —Ben to Luke

"*I*n my experience, there is no such thing as luck."

—Ben to Han

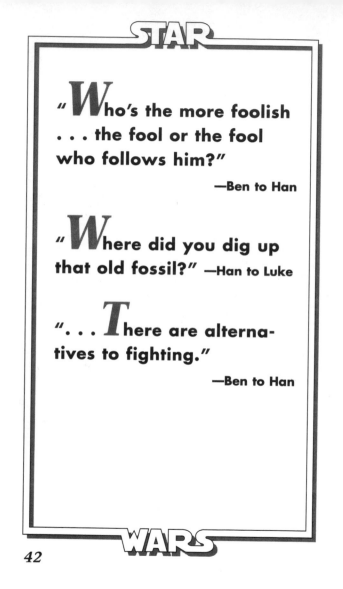

"*W*ho's the more foolish
. . . the fool or the fool
who follows him?"

—Ben to Han

"*W*here did you dig up
that old fossil?" —Han to Luke

". . . *T*here are alterna-
tives to fighting."

—Ben to Han

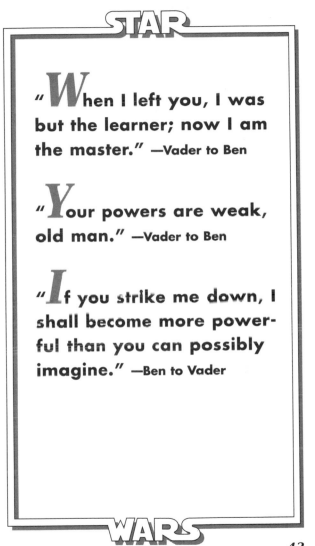

"When I left you, I was but the learner; now I am the master." —Vader to Ben

"Your powers are weak, old man." —Vader to Ben

"If you strike me down, I shall become more powerful than you can possibly imagine." —Ben to Vader

"*L*uke, don't give in to hate—that leads to the dark side." —Ben's spirit to Luke

". . . *Y*ou're going to find that many of the truths we cling to depend greatly on our own point of view."

—Ben's spirit to Luke

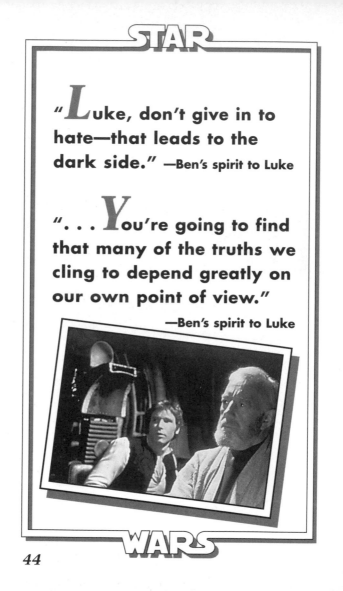

USE THE
FORCE...

"... *T*he Force is what gives a Jedi his power. It's an energy field created by all living things. It surrounds us and penetrates us. It binds the galaxy together." —Ben to Luke

"*T*he ability to destroy a planet is insignificant next to the power of the Force." —Vader to Admiral Motti

"**D**on't try to frighten us with your sorcerer's ways, Lord Vader."

—Admiral Motti to Vader

"**T**hese aren't the droids you're looking for."

—Ben to stormtroopers

"**R**emember, a Jedi can feel the Force flowing through him." —Ben to Luke

"**H**okey religions and ancient weapons are no match for a good blaster at your side, kid."

—Han to Luke

"**T**here's no mystical energy field controls my destiny." —Han

"**Y**our eyes can deceive you. Don't trust them. Stretch out with your feelings." —Ben to Luke

"*T*he Force will be with you . . . always."

—Ben to Luke

"*D*on't underestimate the Force!" —Vader to Tarkin

"*U*se the Force, Luke."

—Ben's spirit

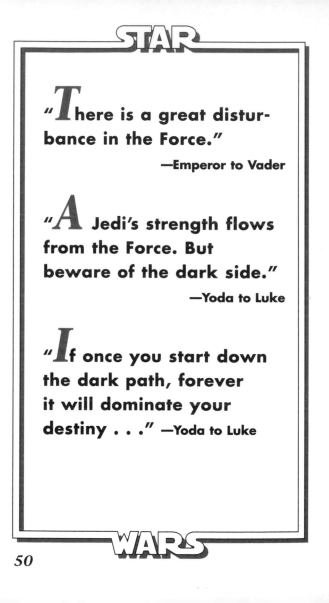

STAR

"*T*here is a great distur-
bance in the Force."

—Emperor to Vader

"*A* Jedi's strength flows
from the Force. But
beware of the dark side."

—Yoda to Luke

"*I*f once you start down
the dark path, forever
it will dominate your
destiny . . ." —Yoda to Luke

WARS

"*A* Jedi uses the Force
for knowledge and
defense—never for
attack." —Yoda to Luke

"... *M*y ally is the
Force, and a powerful ally
it is." —Yoda

"*Y*our mind powers will
not work on me, boy."

—Jabba to Luke

"**S**trike me down with all of your hatred, and your journey towards the dark side will be complete."

—Emperor to Luke

IT'S NOT EASY BEING GREEN

"*I*'m looking for a great warrior." —Luke to Yoda

"*W*ars not make one great." —Yoda

"*A*dventure. Heh! Excitement. Heh! A Jedi craves not these things."
—Yoda to Luke

"*I* cannot teach him. The boy has no patience."
—Yoda to Ben's spirit

"*S*o certain are you.
Always with you it cannot
be done." —Yoda to Luke

"*Y*ou must unlearn what
you have learned."

—Yoda to Luke

"*T*ry not. Do. Or do not.
There is no try."

—Yoda to Luke

"*I* won't fail you—I'm not afraid." —Luke to Yoda

"*O*h, you will be. You will be." —Yoda to Luke

"*S*ize matters not. Look at me. Judge me by my size, do you?" —Yoda to Luke

"*L*uminous beings are we . . . not this crude matter." —Yoda to Luke

"*Y*ou want the impossible." —Luke to Yoda

"*I* don't believe it."

—Luke to Yoda

"*T*hat is why you fail."

—Yoda to Luke

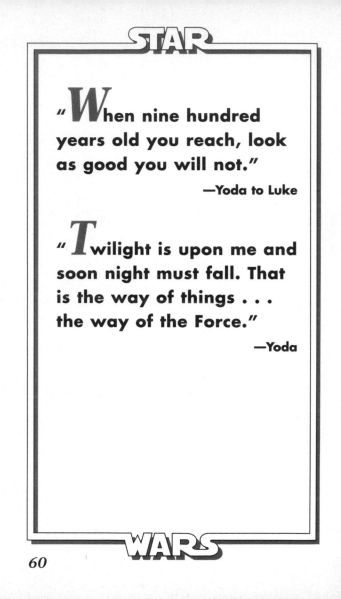

STAR

"*W*hen nine hundred years old you reach, look as good you will not."

—Yoda to Luke

"*T*wilight is upon me and soon night must fall. That is the way of things . . . the way of the Force."

—Yoda

WARS

THE
WALKING
CARPET

*"I*t's not wise to upset a Wookiee." —Han to C-3PO

*"B*ut sir, nobody worries about upsetting a droid."
—C-3PO to Han

*"T*hat's 'cause a droid don't pull people's arms outta their sockets when they lose." —Han to C-3PO

"*I* suggest a new strate-gy, Artoo. Let the Wookiee win." —C-3PO to R2-D2

"*C*ome here, you big coward!" —Han to Chewbacca

"*W*ill somebody get this big walking carpet out of my way!?"—Princess Leia
(concerning Chewbacca)

"*L*augh it up, fuzzball."
—Han to Chewbacca

WARS

"*I*'m backwards, you flea-bitten furball."

—C-3PO to Chewbacca

"*I*'m terribly sorry about all this. After all, he's only a Wookiee." —C-3PO to Lando

"*I* thought that hairy beast would be the end of me." —C-3PO

"*G*reat, Chewie! Great! Always thinking with your stomach." —Han

THE
OTHER
SWASHBUCKLER

"*L*ando Calrissian. He's a card player, gambler, scoundrel. You'd like him." —Han to Leia

"*W*hy you slimy, double-crossing, no-good swindler!" —Lando greeting Han

"*I*'m responsible these days. It's the price you pay for being successful."
—Lando

"**Y**ou fixed us all real good, didn't you? My friend! —Han to Lando

"... *I* got my own problems." —Lando to Han

"*Y*ou certainly have a way with people."

—Leia to Lando

FATHER
AND SON

"**Y**our father wanted you
to have this when you
were old enough. . . ."

—Ben to Luke (concerning the
lightsaber)

"**M**uch anger in him,
like his father."

—Yoda (concerning Luke)

"**I** am your father."

—Vader to Luke

STAR

"*J*oin me, and together we can rule the galaxy as father and son."

—Vader to Luke

WARS

"*I* know there is good in you. The Emperor hasn't driven it from you fully."
—Luke to Vader

"*S*earch your feelings, Father. . . . Let go of your hate." —Luke to Vader

"*I*t is pointless to resist, my son." —Vader to Luke

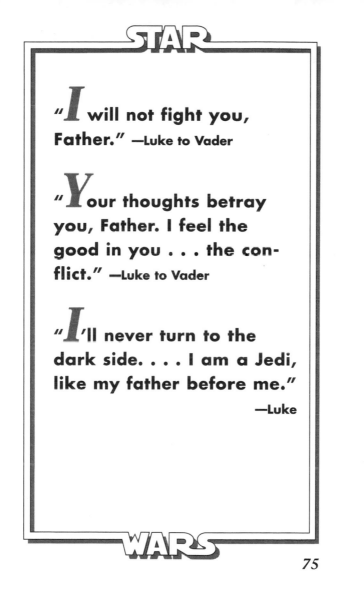

"*I* will not fight you,
Father." —Luke to Vader

"*Y*our thoughts betray
you, Father. I feel the
good in you . . . the con-
flict." —Luke to Vader

"*I*'ll never turn to the
dark side. . . . I am a Jedi,
like my father before me."
—Luke

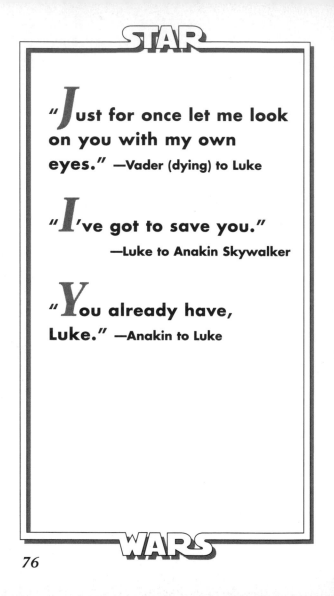

"*J*ust for once let me look on you with my own eyes." —Vader (dying) to Luke

"*I*'ve got to save you." —Luke to Anakin Skywalker

"*Y*ou already have, Luke." —Anakin to Luke

HEARTS
AND
FLOWERS

"*L*ook, I ain't in this for your revolution, and I'm not in it for you, Princess. . . . I'm in it for the money!" —Han to Leia

". . . *D*on't get all mushy on me." —Han to Leia

"*A*fraid I was going to leave without giving you a good-bye kiss?"

—Han to Leia

"*I*'d just as soon kiss a Wookiee." —Leia to Han

"*I* think you just can't bear to let a gorgeous guy like me out of your sight."
—Han to Leia

"*I* don't know where you get your delusions, laser brain." —Leia to Han

"*C*aptain, being held by you isn't quite enough to get me excited." —Leia to Han

"*S*orry, sweetheart. We haven't got time for anything else." —Han to Leia

"*Y*ou like me because I'm a scoundrel. There aren't enough scoundrels in your life." —Han to Leia

"*I* happen to like nice men." —Leia

"*I*'m a nice man." —Han

"*N*o, you're not." —Leia

"*I* love you!" —Leia to Han

"*I* know." —Han to Leia

"*I* love you." —Han to Leia

"*I* know." —Leia to Han

JABBA'S RULES OF GOOD BUSINESS

"**W**hat if everyone who smuggled for me dropped their cargo at the first sign of an Imperial starship?"

—Jabba to Han

"**J**abba, you're a wonderful human being."

—Han to Jabba

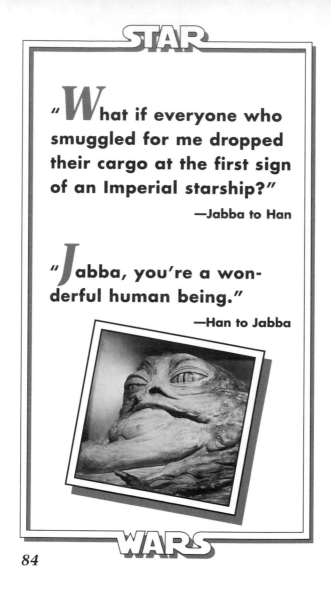

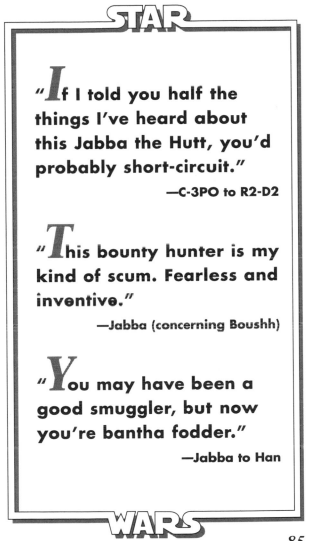

"*I*f I told you half the things I've heard about this Jabba the Hutt, you'd probably short-circuit."

—C-3PO to R2-D2

"*T*his bounty hunter is my kind of scum. Fearless and inventive."

—Jabba (concerning Boushh)

"*Y*ou may have been a good smuggler, but now you're bantha fodder."

—Jabba to Han

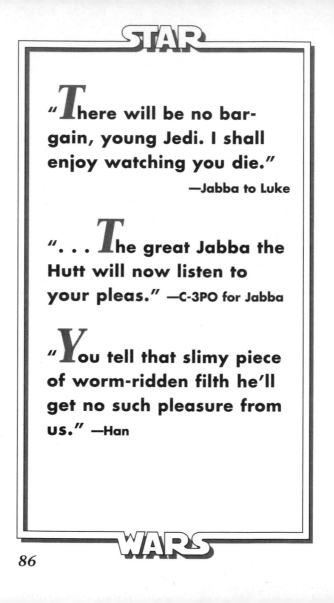

"*T*here will be no bar-
gain, young Jedi. I shall
enjoy watching you die."
—Jabba to Luke

". . . *T*he great Jabba the
Hutt will now listen to
your pleas." —C-3PO for Jabba

"*Y*ou tell that slimy piece
of worm-ridden filth he'll
get no such pleasure from
us." —Han

RESPONSIBILITY

"It's not my fault!"

—C-3PO

"It's not my fault!"

—Lando Calrissian

"It's not my fault!"

—Han Solo

INTERPLANETARY RELATIONS

"*T*his is a consular ship. We're on a diplomatic mission." —Rebel officer to Vader

"*D*on't act so surprised, Your Highness. You weren't on any mercy mission this time." —Vader to Leia

"*F*ear will keep the local systems in line. Fear of this battle station."

—Tarkin (concerning the Death Star)

"*T*his will be a day long remembered. It has seen the end of Kenobi and will soon see the end of the Rebellion." —Vader

"*E*vacuate? In our moment of triumph? I think you overestimate their chances!" —Tarkin

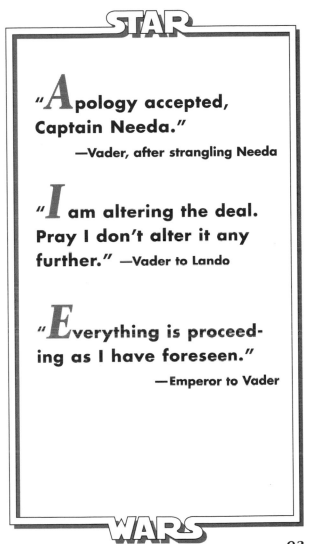

"**A**pology accepted, Captain Needa."

—Vader, after strangling Needa

"**I** am altering the deal. Pray I don't alter it any further." —Vader to Lando

"**E**verything is proceeding as I have foreseen."

—Emperor to Vader

"*T*hey'll have that shield down on time . . . or this'll be the shortest offensive of all time."

—Lando

"*F*reeze! You Rebel scum!" —Imperial officer to Han

ALL THE BEST VACATION SPOTS

"I've got such a bad case of dust contamination, I can barely move." —C-3PO

*". . . I*f there's a bright center to the universe, you're on the planet that it's farthest from."
—Luke to C-3PO (concerning Tatooine)

*"T*he Jundland Wastes are not to be traveled lightly." —Ben

"**M**os Eisley Spaceport. You will never find a more wretched hive of scum and villainy." —Ben

"... **W**atch your step. This place can be a little rough."

—Ben (concerning the Cantina)

"**T**here isn't enough life on this ice cube to fill a space cruiser."

—Han Solo (concerning Hoth)

"*Y*our tauntaun'll freeze before you reach the first marker." —Rebel to Han Solo

"*T*hen I'll see you in Hell." —Han Solo to Rebel

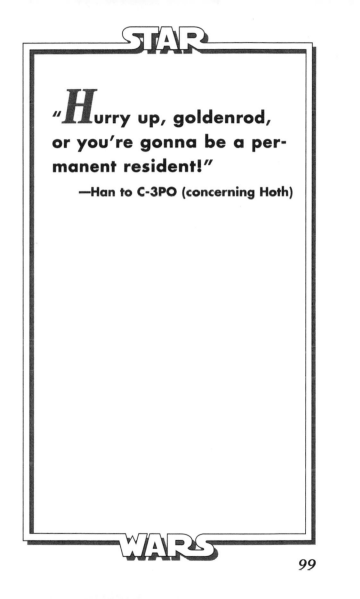

STAR

"*H*urry up, goldenrod, or you're gonna be a permanent resident!"

—Han to C-3PO (concerning Hoth)

WARS

"**O**h, I told you it was dangerous here."

—C-3PO
(concerning the Moon of Endor)

FEELINGS

STAR

"*I* have a very bad feeling about this."

—Luke Skywalker

"*I* got a bad feeling
about this." —Han Solo

"*I* have a bad feeling
about this." —Princess Leia

WARS

STAR

"*A*rtoo, I have a bad feeling about this." —C-3PO

"*I* have a really bad feeling about this." —Han Solo

WARS

About the Author

In two decades Steve Sansweet transformed a modest hobby into the world's largest private collection of Star Wars memorabilia. And he recently gave up a life-long journalism career to join Lucasfilm as its Director of Specialty Marketing to promote Star Wars to fans everywhere.

Born in Philadelphia, Sansweet got his bachelor's degree from Temple University, and was named outstanding graduate in journalism. He was a feature writer for the *Philadelphia Inquirer* before joining *The Wall Street Journal*. He transferred to Los Angeles where he wrote on topics ranging from multinational corporate bribery to the civil rights of mental patients, and for three years covered Hollywood. He served as the *Journal*'s Los Angeles bureau chief for nine year starting in March 1987.

Sansweet has written *The Punishment Cure* (1976); *Science Fiction Toys and Models* (1980); *Star Wars: From Concept to Screen Collectible* (1992); and *Tomart's Price Guide to Star Wars Collectibles* (1994). He is working on *The Star Wars Encyclopedia* for Del Rey. The Southern California resident writes Star Wars columns and trading-card backs, and has co-hosted numerous QVC Star Wars collectibles shows.

A fan above all else, he can't wait until the premiere of the next trilogy.